CAMILLA
THE
TAIL - WAGGING
TUTOR

Written by:
Jennifer Brandt

Illustrated by:
Carolyn Williams

Jennifer Brandt, Camilla the Tail-Wagging Tutor.
Copyright ©2024 by Jennifer Brandt

Illustrations by Carolyn Williams
Cover layout and book design by Carolyn Williams
www.carolynwilliamsart.com

Published by KWE Publishing: www.kwepub.com

ISBN: 979-8-9918596-0-8
Library of Congress Control Number: 2024924001

Dedicated to Cesar, an incredible therapy dog
who helped hundreds of kids and adults in his short life.
He was the first dog I trained to be a therapy dog and was
my inspiration for Camilla to become one. Camilla continues
Cesar's legacy and his life's work volunteering in hospitals,
nursing homes, and schools.

One beautiful spring day,
    the letter Camilla had been waiting for finally arrived.

Jennifer, her dog mama, read it out loud.

"Congratulations! You have successfully completed
your dog training course and are ready to become a
READING TUTOR."

Camilla wagged her tail and ran in happy circles.
She was going to read with children
at Cleveland Elementary School!

But would she remember everything she had learned?
She repeated the rules to herself:

Lie quietly.

Let the children pet her.

No slobbering.

Camilla was determined
to be the best
tail-wagging tutor
Cleveland Elementary
School had ever seen.

There was a knock at the door. Jennifer's two nieces,
Aubree and Paisley, had stopped over for a visit.

"Hi, Auntie!" said Aubree as she gave Jennifer a hug.

Camilla ran over and jumped up on Paisley.

"No, Camilla," said Jennifer. "No jumping."

Camilla lay on the floor and put her head down. Would she remember that tail-wagging tutors could not jump at school?

Camilla heard Jennifer say to Paisley and Aubree, "Guess what? Camilla passed her dog training course and is officially a reading tutor. Both of you, and the kids at your school, can take turns reading to her."

Camilla couldn't wait. She loved stories, and she loved kids.

Paisley squeezed Camilla tightly. She couldn't wait for Camilla's visit either. "You are going to do so good," Paisley told her.

When Aubree and Paisley left, Camilla again started
thinking about all the school rules. No jumping.
No slobbering. No barking. No running. So many things for
a dog *not* to do! But Camilla wanted to be the best
tail-wagging tutor the school had ever seen, so she would
try really hard to follow all the rules.

A week flew by, and her first day of school was here.
Camilla took her bath,

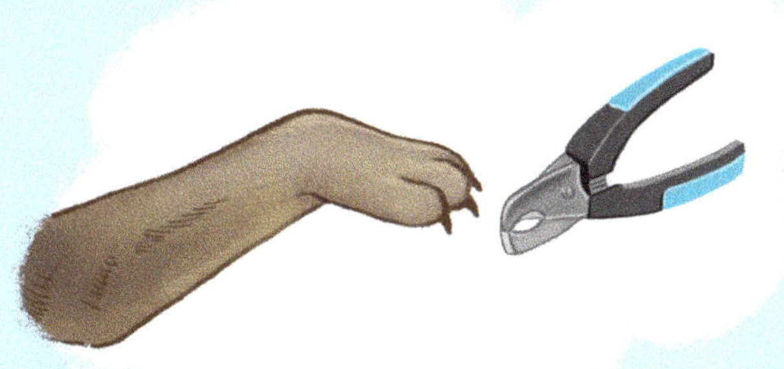

had her nails trimmed,

and even her teeth brushed.

She was looking her best and ready for readers.

Oooooh, Camilla thought to herself, I want to jump right now, but there is no jumping at school.
LIBRARY

As Jennifer and Camilla walked in the school's front door, Camilla's tail wagged with excitement.

The principal greeted them in the office and showed them to the library.

Camilla reminded herself, *No running.*

The first student came into the library. Liam walked right up to Jennifer and asked, "Can your dog really talk?"

Jennifer smiled and replied, "Camilla can speak by barking, but she is trained not to. She's going to listen to you read your book about baseball."

"Ooooh! I thought *Camilla* was reading to *me*!" said Liam.
"I get it now."

Liam opened his book and began reading about baseball
and telling Camilla how much he loved the sport.

Camilla sat there quietly as he petted her and read.

The next student, Ryan, came running across the library to the carpet where Camilla was sitting. Camilla stood up, and her tail was wagging fast.

Ryan jumped up and said, "Hi, Camilla. My name is Ryan."

Camilla was excited, so she jumped too.

Jennifer immediately said,

When Camilla landed back on her feet, she remembered that she was not supposed to jump or bark and feared she would be asked to leave. Camilla could see the disappointment on the faces of the teacher and Jennifer, so she sat down on the library carpet.

Jennifer told Ryan, "Why don't you sit next to Camilla and
read her your book about caterpillars?"

Ryan did just that, and Camilla sat quietly for the remainder of the story. She did it! She was able to sit and keep quiet even though she was excited.

Julianne came to the library next and walked very quickly
to sit on the carpet, almost sitting on Camilla's head.

Julianne brought a book about dogs. As she began reading
the book, she put her hand on Camilla's head and pushed her
face in the direction of the book. "Camilla needs to be able
to see the pictures."

Camilla remembered what she learned in her training class.
Instead of being upset that a child pushed her face, she gave
out a big sigh, looked up at Julianne, and then laid her head
in Julianne's lap. Julianne was so happy and loved how snuggly
Camilla was. She no longer cared if Camilla was looking at the
pages as she loved snuggling with her new furry friend.

The last girl came into the library with her teacher,
Mrs Cooper. Her name was Annie. Mrs. Cooper walked over
to Jennifer and said, "Annie is very nervous to read out loud
and refuses to in class. I am hoping Camilla can help."

Jennifer guided Annie to sit next to Camilla. "Annie, I see you
brought a book about kangaroos. Camilla does not know
anything about kangaroos. Would you like to read it to her?"

Annie shook her head no, still not speaking any words.

Camilla looked right at Annie with her sweet eyes. She didn't understand why this girl was sitting next to her but would not open her book and read it.

Jennifer said, "Did you know that Camilla cannot read the words?"

Annie looked up with a confused face. "She can't? I thought she was a reading dog?"

"She is," replied Jennifer. "Camilla is trained to just listen to you. If you make a mistake, she will not know."

Annie was relieved and smiled. Camilla could sense her happiness and started wagging her tail, hoping to hear another story.

Annie opened her book, read a few words, and then stopped to look at Camilla. Camilla was lying on her side enjoying Annie's book about kangaroos. Annie read a few more words out loud and looked at Camilla again. Camilla had not moved. "She really does listen," said Annie.

Annie continued to read, finishing the entire book. As she closed the final page, she smiled. "I did it. I read the whole book!" Annie reached over to Camilla and petted her belly. Camilla rolled all the way on her back, putting her feet in the air so Annie could scratch her belly.

The end of the day was here, and it was time for Camilla
and Jennifer to go home.

The principal met Camilla and Jennifer at the school exit
doors. "Thank you for coming today; the children loved her
and are already asking when she can come back." The principal
asked, "Would you be willing to come back every week? We
would love to have you!"

Camilla's tail wagged, and she went in circles. "From the look
on Camilla's face, I can tell she would *love* to come back and
help the kids weekly to practice their reading skills!"

Camilla had done it! She remembered all the rules she needed to follow. She was the best tail-wagging tutor ever, and she could not wait to go back!

Camilla's Author Note

Hi! My name is Camilla, and this is a story of my adventures as a therapy dog.

Therapy dogs are dogs who go with their owners to volunteer in settings such as schools, hospitals, and nursing homes.

From working with a child who is learning to read to visiting a senior in assisted living, therapy dogs and their owners work together as a team to improve the lives of other people.

I had to pass a very difficult and challenging obedience and temperament test before I was given my license in April 2017. I will have you know that I passed the test with flying colors.

Nothing fills my heart more than seeing the smiles on everyone's faces when I arrive.

I have enjoyed the kids reading to me at the elementary school more than any of my other pastimes. I love hearing all the stories and constantly being loved on.

Outside of my work as a therapy dog, I love snuggles in a nice warm bed, sunbathing on a warm day, playing with my beloved ball, and digging holes. I know my owner is not too happy about me digging holes, but I soooo love it!

I feel very lucky to have found my owner as I am living my best doggie life!

Love,

Camilla 

I grew up loving animals as a
young girl in Wisconsin. I have been
an entrepreneur, operating my own
Mary Kay business since 2005.
As a working human and dog mom,
I was inspired by my furry BFF,
Camilla, to write my first
children's book.

The star of this book, Camilla, was
adopted by me just before the age
of one after a rough road at the local
humane society and foster homes.
Camilla was very shy and was nervous
around people. After having lots of
positive experiences with people and
other dogs, Camilla grew into the
kind, confident, sweet soul that she is.

Camilla and I visit schools as part of Therapy Dogs International's Tail Waggin'
Tutors program. During our visits to school, children read books to Camilla,
who politely listens and never interrupts. It has been exceptionally rewarding.
One of my favorite experiences was when a young girl skipped several pages
while reading a book because the story included a bear, and the girl was worried
Camilla would be scared. It was precious!

While I lived in North Carolina and Virginia, I still call Wisconsin my home.
I live in the small town of Cleveland, Wisconsin, with my husband Kurt, son
Tuck, Camilla, and two other furbaby dogs, Chet and Levi.

Camilla and I hope you enjoy this story and share it with your family and friends.
~ Jennifer

Camilla the
Tail-Wagging Tutor
in action with
the students at
Cleveland Elementary
School!